THE
LITTLE KITCHEN
COLLECTION

THE

BREAD

COOKBOOK

Judith Ferguson

ILLUSTRATED BY AISLINN ADAMS

HarperCollins*Publishers*

First published in 1993 by
The Appletree Press Ltd

THE BREAD COOKBOOK

HarperCollins books may be purchased for
educational, business, or sales promotional use.
For information please write: Special Markets
Department, HarperCollins Publishers, Inc.,
10 East 53rd Street, New York, NY 10022.

FIRST EDITION

LIBRARY OF CONGRESS CATALOG CARD NUMBER:

92-52578

ISBN 0-06-016901-X

93 94 95 96 97 10 9 8 7 6 5 4 3 2 1

Introduction

Few things equal the tantalizing aroma of freshly baked bread. Baking a beautiful loaf of bread can make you feel very pleased with yourself. And why not? Breadmaking is a satisfying experience that really brings you in touch with what cooking is all about. It can be an opportunity to relax and let stress just disappear while being creative at the same time.

The only problem is deciding what kind of bread to bake as there are so many different varieties from all over the world. Breads fall into two main categories, though. Quick breads are so called because they need no rising time, relying on the action of baking powder or baking soda. These breads need to go into the oven as soon as they are mixed.

Yeast breads take a little longer, but with the arrival of fast action yeast, even these breads are quicker to make than you might think. Both fresh and active dry yeasts need to be mixed with lukewarm liquid before being added to the dry ingredients, but fast action yeast goes right in with the flour. After kneading, shape the bread immediately so it needs only one rising. Almost any recipe can be adapted to use fast action yeast. Most breads freeze well, too.

In American culinary history there are so many unusual and exceptionally good breads that this book could be at least twice as long. Many of these breads reflect their European ancestry, but some, like corn bread and sourdough bread, are typically American. Above all, the recipes are fun and rewarding to make, so roll up your sleeves, set the oven and get baking!

A note on measures

All spoon measurements are level unless otherwise stated. Unless specified, the eggs called for are graded "large". Bear in mind that "extra-large" eggs will alter the liquid measurements slightly. Flour can absorb moisture from the atmosphere, so in rainy or very humid weather you may find you need to add a bit more.

Sourdough Starters

Once these starter mixtures begin to ferment, they bubble up to about twice their volume, so be sure to start them in large enough containers and don't cover them too tightly.

Yeast Starter

> *1 pkg active dry yeast*
> *2 cups warm water*
> *2 cups all-purpose flour*
> **(4 cups approx.)**

Mix yeast, water and flour in a food processor or by hand. Place in a large container. Leave in a warm place, loosely covered, to ferment for up to 48 hours. The longer it stands, the stronger the sourdough taste will be. It can be stored in the refrigerator. Keep it going by feeding it once a week with 1 cup all-purpose flour, ¼ cup sugar, and 1 cup warm milk. It will grow considerably after being fed.

Potato Starter

> *4 cups all-purpose flour (or use wholewheat*
> *or buckwheat flour, if liked)*
> *1 cup sugar*
> *½ cup mashed potatoes*
> *4 cups potato cooking water*
> **(6–8 cups)**

Combine flour, sugar, mashed potatoes and cooking water. Substitute plain warm water, if using leftover mashed potatoes. Beat until fairly smooth, then pour into a large container. Cover loosely and leave in a warm place for about 48 hours. Mixture will bubble a lot during the first 36 hours, then subside slightly. It will smell like vodka, but that's normal!

Swedish Rye Brea[d]

Also known as Limpa, this bread gets its u[...]
a hint of orange and the mild liqorice tast[e...]

1½ pkgs active dry yea[st]
¾ cup warm water
¼ cup molasses
1½ tbsps brown sug[ar]
1 tsp salt
2 tbsps melted butter or m[argarine]
grated peel of 1 oran[ge]
1¼ cups rye flou[r]
2 tsps aniseed or fenne[l seed]
1¼ cups all-purpose [flour]
(1 loaf)

Preheat oven to 375°F. Mix yeast an[d ...]
sugar, salt, 1 tablespoon butter or ma[rgarine ...]
flour and aniseed or fennel seed. Mix [...]
add enough white flour to make a sof[t ...]
firm enough to knead.

Knead on a lightly-floured surfac[e ...]
until smooth and elastic. Try not to [...]
flour. Place dough in a greased bow[l ...]
in a warm place until doubled, abo[ut ...]

Punch down the dough and shap[e ...]
loaf. Place on a greased baking sh[eet ...]
top. Cover and leave to rise again u[...]

Brush the top of the loaf with t[...]
or margarine and bake about 30 to [...]
sounds hollow on the bottom wh[en ...]
rack.

Sourdough Cheese and Dill Buns

Try these the next time you make hamburgers. They'll make all other buns seem run-of-the-mill. They'll be popular, though, no matter what sandwich fillings you use.

1½ cups wholewheat flour
1½–2 cups all-purpose flour
1½ tbsps sugar
1 tsp salt
½ tsp baking soda
1 pkg fast action yeast
1¼ cups grated sharp Cheddar
1 tbsp chopped dill
4 tbsps melted margarine
1 egg
1 cup sourdough starter
at room temperature (see p. 4)
vegetable oil
(makes 12)

Preheat oven to 375°F. Combine the flours. Add sugar, salt, soda and yeast. Reserve ½ cup of the cheese and add the rest with dill to the dry ingredients. Make a well in the middle and add the margarine, egg and sourdough starter. Mix to a soft dough and add any remaining flour as necessary.

Knead on a floured surface for about 10 minutes until smooth and elastic. Divide into 12 pieces, shape into smooth rounds, and flatten into bun shapes. Place on greased baking sheets and brush with oil. Cover loosely and leave to rise about 1 hour or until doubled in size. Sprinkle the tops with the reserved cheese. Bake about 20 minutes and remove immediately to wire racks to cool.

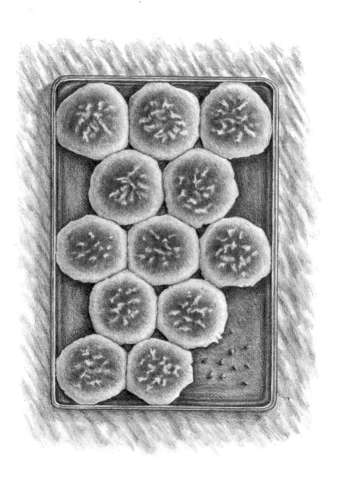

Soft Pretzels

These snacks of German origin are now typical street food in New York. They're best eaten warm, spread with a little spicy mustard. It's the unusual method of boiling the shaped dough in water and soda before baking that gives pretzels their characteristic flavor.

2 cups all-purpose flour	*6 tbsps baking soda*
1½ tsps fast action yeast	*beaten egg to glaze*
⅔ cup warm water	*coarse salt*
3 pts water	

(makes 8–10)

Preheat oven to 425°F. Mix flour, yeast, sugar and salt. Stir in ⅔ cup warm water until well blended. Add more flour, if necessary to make a soft dough or a little more warm water if the dough is too dry. Knead about 10 minutes on a floured surface and divide into 8 or 10 even-size pieces. Roll each into a thin rope about 12 inches long. To form pretzel shapes, pick up the ends of the dough ropes and form into loops that cross over each other in the middle. Tuck the ends under and press to stick them down.

Place on very well-oiled baking sheets. Cover with well-oiled plastic wrap or paper, or with a well-floured towel. Leave in a warm place until doubled in size, at least 40 minutes. Refrigerate until firm, if desired, to make the pretzels easier to move.

Meanwhile bring the water and soda to the boil in a large, deep frying pan. Lower the heat until water is gently bubbling. Remove pretzels from the baking sheets with an oiled spatula and slide them one at a time into the water. Cook 3 or 4 at a time depending on the pan's size. Drain, return to the greased baking sheet. When all the pretzels are cooked, brush them with beaten egg and sprinkle over with coarse salt. Bake about 10 minutes or until golden brown. Don't let them overbake. Serve warm.

Sourdough Buckwheat Biscuits

Buckwheat flour has a nutty flavor and, with its dark flecks, makes attractive breads. If you use buckwheat or wholewheat flour to make your starter, use all-purpose flour in this recipe, otherwise the biscuits will be too heavy.

1 cup buckwheat flour
³/₄ tsp baking soda
¹/₄ tsp salt
¹/₃ cup vegetable oil
1 cup sourdough starter
(makes 24)

Preheat oven 350°F. Lightly grease 2 or 3 baking sheets. Combine flour, soda, salt and make a well in the middle of the ingredients. Pour in the oil and sourdough starter. Mix to thick dropping consistency. Drop dough by spoonfuls onto the baking sheets. Bake immediately for about 10 minutes or until pale golden brown. These biscuits will dry out very quickly, if overbaked. Serve warm.

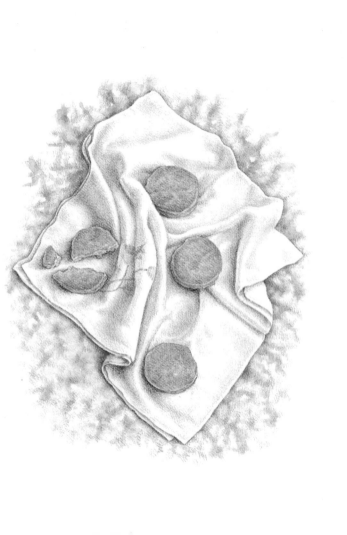

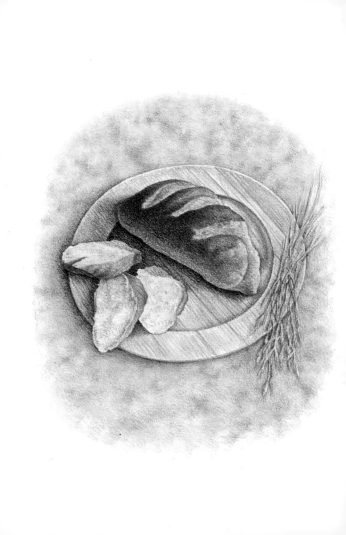

Sourdough Bread

Some say that sourdough bread can't be made successfully outside San Francisco, but even sceptics will agree this loaf is very close to the real thing.

1 cup warm water
1 pkg active dry yeast
1 tbsp sugar
2 tsps salt
1½ cups sourdough starter
4–5 cups all-purpose flour
cornmeal

Preheat oven to 325°F. Mix water and yeast. Stir in sugar, salt, and sourdough starter. Beat in 4 cups flour. Add enough remaining flour to make a soft dough. Knead on a floured surface, working in more flour, if necessary, until dough is smooth and elastic.

Place in a greased bowl, cover and leave in a warm place to rise until doubled. Punch down and shape dough into two long loaves, thicker in the middle and tapered at the ends. Sprinkle two baking sheets with cornmeal and place on the loaves. Make several diagonal cuts across the tops, cover loosely and leave to rise again about 20 minutes.

Bake loaves 40 to 45 minutes, or until they sound hollow when tapped. For a shiny crust, brush with a mixture of beaten egg and a pinch of salt about halfway through baking.

Potato Caraway Loaf

Mashed potato gives bread dough a very light and tender texture. Omit the caraway seeds if you don't like them, or use poppy seeds instead. This dough also makes delicious rolls.

2 pkgs active dry yeast
1½ cups cooking water from the potatoes
1 cup mashed potatoes
¼ cup sugar
2 tsps salt
2 eggs, beaten
7–8 cups all-purpose flour
⅔ cup vegetable shortening, melted
1 tbsp caraway seeds
milk
(makes 2 loaves or 48 rolls)

Preheat oven to 400°F. Mix yeast with cooking water. If using leftover mashed potatoes, use warm water instead. Add mashed potatoes, sugar, salt and eggs and mix thoroughly. Add about half the flour and mix well. Beat in the shortening, caraway seeds and enough of the remaining flour to make a soft, but not sticky, dough. Knead on a floured surface for about 10 minutes until smooth and elastic. Place dough in a greased bowl, cover and leave in a warm place for about 1½ hours, or until doubled.

Punch down the dough and knead into 2 large loaves or shape into about 48 rolls. Place in greased pans or on greased baking sheets. Cover loosely and leave to rise again until doubled, about 30 minutes. Brush with milk or dust with flour, if desired. Bake about 20 to 25 minutes, or until loaves sound hollow when tapped. Bake rolls at 425°F for 10 to 15 minutes. Remove immediately to cool on wire racks.

Bagels

Poaching the dough in water before baking is what gives bagels their texture – chewy inside, crusty outside. Traditional with lox (smoked salmon) and cream cheese, they're equally good with just about any sandwich filling you can think of, or just toasted and spread with butter or cream cheese.

1½ cups warm water	4 qts water
2 pkgs active dry yeast	1 tbsp sugar
1 tsp salt	2 egg whites, lightly beaten
2 tbsps sugar	poppy seeds (optional)
4–5 cups all-purpose flour	

(makes 12)

Preheat oven to 375°F. Mix warm water and yeast. Combine salt, sugar and 4 cups of the flour and make a well in the middle. Pour in the yeast mixture and mix to a soft dough. Add more flour as necessary until dough is just firm enough to handle. Knead for about 10 minutes, cover and leave to rest for about 15 minutes. Divide into 12 pieces. Roll each into a rope about 7 inches long. Form into doughnut rings. Dampen ends and pinch together to seal. Alternatively, shape into smooth rounds and poke a hole in the middle of each with your finger, pulling gently to enlarge each hole. Leave on greased baking sheets, cover loosely and allow to rise for 20 to 30 minutes or until puffy. Refrigerate until firm, if desired, to make them easier to move.

Bring water and sugar to the boil in a large deep pan, then lower heat to simmering. Drop in about 4 bagels at a time. Cook about 3 minutes per side, turning once. Drain and return to the greased baking sheets. Brush with egg white and sprinkle with poppy seeds. Bake 30 to 35 minutes.

Cottage Cheese Pinwheels

These rolls are a snack in themselves. Be sure to use small curd cottage cheese for easier blending and a creamier filling.

2½ cups all-purpose flour
1 tsp sugar
1 tsp salt
1 pkg fast action yeast
½ cup margarine, melted
1 cup small-curd cottage cheese
1 egg, beaten

Filling:

3 tbsps margarine, softened
½ cup small-curd cottage cheese
1 tbsp chopped chives
coarsely ground black pepper

(**makes 8–10**)

Preheat oven to 400°F. Mix flour, sugar, salt, and yeast. Make a well in the middle and add the margarine, cottage cheese, and egg. Mix to a dough, adding more flour until it is firm enough to knead. Knead about 10 minutes on a floured surface. Roll out to a square about 14 inches.

Spread with softened margarine and then cover evenly with cottage cheese and chives to within about ½ inch of the edges. Sprinkle with a little pepper. Roll up tightly and cut into 8 to 10 slices. Place cut side up in a greased 8 inches square or round pan. Cover loosely and leave in a warm place to rise, about 1 hour. Bake 10 to 15 minutes or until lightly browned.

Dark Rye Bread

Deli sandwiches would not be the same without this bread! Try to add as little extra flour as possible during kneading because the softer the dough, the better the bread will be.

1¹/₂ pkgs active dry yeast
³/₄ cup warm water
¹/₄ cup molasses
1 tbsp shortening, melted
1 ¹/₃ cups rye flour
1 ¹/₃ cups all-purpose flour
1 tsp salt
1 tbsp caraway seeds
oil
cornmeal

Preheat oven to 375°F. Mix the yeast and water and leave it to dissolve. Stir in the molasses and melted shortening. Combine the two flours, salt, and caraway seeds. Pour the yeast mixture into the middle of the flour and mix to a soft dough. Knead on a lightly floured surface for about 10 minutes or until dough is smooth and springs back when touched. Place in a greased bowl and cover. Leave in a warm place to rise for about 2 hours.

Lightly grease a baking sheet and sprinkle with cornmeal. Punch down the dough and shape it into one round. Flatten the top slightly. Brush the top with oil and cover loosely. Leave to rise again, 40 minutes to 1 hour. Sprinkle very lightly with cornmeal and bake about 30 to 40 minutes or until the bread sounds hollow on the bottom when tapped. Cool on a wire rack.

Foccacia

This Italian flatbread is now popular everywhere. It's very versatile, you can bake it plain or with lots of interesting additions. It makes a great pizza base, too.

1 pkg active dry yeast
5 tbsps olive oil
1¼ cups warm water
4 cups all-purpose flour
1 tsp salt
1 tsp sugar
fresh basil leaves, chopped garlic, rosemary leaves,
sun-dried tomatoes, pitted black olives,
grated Parmesan cheese, coarse salt
(1 loaf)

Preheat oven to 400°F. Combine yeast, olive oil, and water. Mix flour, salt, and sugar and pour in the yeast mixture. Mix to a soft dough. Knead for about 10 minutes on a floured surface. Place in a greased bowl, cover and leave to rise for about 1 hour or until doubled.

Punch down the dough and divide in thirds. Knead in the flavoring ingredients in whatever combination you like. If using either Parmesan cheese or coarse salt, sprinkle on just before baking. Shape into 3 oblongs about ½ inch thick. Place on oiled baking sheets and press surface very firmly with your finger to make "dimples". Cover loosely and leave to rise until almost doubled, about 30 minutes. Brush with olive oil. Bake about 20 minutes or until breads sound hollow when tapped.

Variation: For pizza bases, pat dough into the pans and cover with toppings before leaving to rise the second time for 15 to 20 minutes. Bake at 425°F for 15 to 20 minutes depending on size.

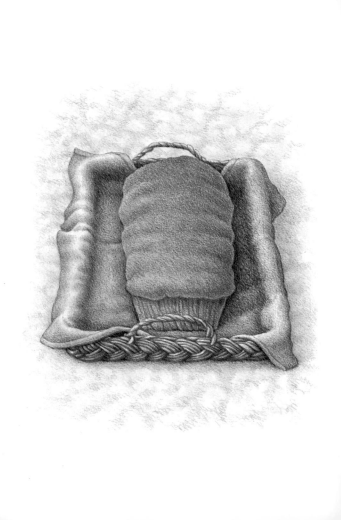

Anadama Bread

There are many tales surrounding the name of this bread. One has it that Anna, "damn her," made a fine bread, or so said her husband. Another has it that the same husband was left to bake his own bread which provoked the comment "Anna, damn her!"

1 1/2 cups boiling water
1/3 cup yellow cornmeal
1 tsp salt
1 1/2 tbsps butter or margarine
1/3 cup molasses
1 pkg active dry yeast
1/4 cup warm water
4–5 cups all-purpose flour

Preheat oven to 375°F. Beat the boiling water into the cornmeal in a large pan with the salt, butter or margarine, and molasses until smooth. Bring just to the boil, stirring constantly. Cool until lukewarm, stirring occasionally. Mix yeast and warm water and stir into the cornmeal. Beat in 4 cups of the flour to form a slightly sticky dough. Add a bit more flour, if absolutely necessary.

Transfer to a greased bowl, cover and leave to rise in a warm place for about 1 1/2 hours, then knead about 10 minutes with as little of the remaining flour as possible. Shape into a loaf and place in a well-greased 9 x 5 inch pan. Brush top lightly with melted butter and loosely cover. Leave to rise again for about 1 hour or until doubled. Bake loaf for about 40 to 50 minutes or until the top is firm and sounds hollow when tapped. Loosen from the pan after 10 minutes, then place on a wire rack. Serve warm with butter or cream cheese.

Beer Braid

Shape this dough anyway you like, but a braided loaf is always attractive. If you can't find dill seeds, caraway or poppy seeds would be good, too. Use dark beer for a richer flavor and color. Delicious for sandwiches.

1³/₄ cups all-purpose flour
1³/₄ cups wholewheat flour
1 pkg fast action yeast
1 tbsp brown sugar
1 tsp salt
1 tbsp dill seeds
1 cup warm beer
¹/₂ cup warm water
2¹/₂ tbsps oil
beaten egg
(1 loaf)

Preheat oven to 375°F. Combine the two flours, yeast, sugar, salt, and dill seeds in a large bowl. Mix beer, water, and oil and pour into the dry ingredients. Beat until dough begins to come together, then knead on a floured surface until smooth and elastic, about 10 minutes. Knead in more flour as necessary, about ¹/₄ cup. Divide dough in thirds and shape each piece into a rope about 14 inches long. Start braiding the ropes together in the middle, then work to both ends. Place on a greased baking sheet and tuck the ends under. Cover loosely and leave to rise in a warm place until about doubled. Brush the top with beaten egg and sprinkle with more dill seeds, if desired. Bake about 35 or 40 minutes, or until bottom sounds hollow when tapped. Cool on a wire rack.

Sour Cream and Chive Bread

Two favorite toppings for baked potatoes combined in a bread that's perfect with salads, soups and appetizers.

1 pkg active dry yeast
¼ cup warm water
½ cup sour cream, at room temperature
3 tbsps melted margarine
2 tbsps sugar
1 tsp salt
1 tbsp chopped chives
1 egg, at room temperature
2–3 cups white flour
beaten egg to glaze
(1 loaf)

Preheat oven to 375°F. Mix yeast and water until well blended. Add sour cream, margarine, sugar, salt, chives, and egg. Beat in about 2 cups of the flour, then add more to make a soft dough. Knead on a well-floured surface until smooth and elastic, about 10 minutes. Place in a greased bowl, cover and leave to rise in a warm place until doubled in bulk, about 1 hour.

Grease a 9 x 5 inch loaf pan. Punch down the dough and knead it into a loaf shape. Place in the greased pan, cover and leave to rise about 20 to 30 minutes. Brush the bread with beaten egg and bake for about 35 minutes or until the loaf sounds hollow when tapped. Remove from the pan and cool on a wire rack.

Fried Yeast Biscuits

These biscuits are golden and light, something like savory doughnuts without the holes! Serve them the same way you would biscuits baked in the oven.

1 pkg active dry yeast
¹/₄ cup warm water
1¹/₂ tbsps lard
³/₄ cup milk
1¹/₂ tbsps sugar
1¹/₂ tsps salt
1³/₄–2¹/₄ cups all-purpose flour
vegetable oil for frying
(makes 12–14)

Mix yeast and water and leave until dissolved. Heat the lard and milk until lukewarm. Stir in the sugar. Combine salt and ³/₄ cup flour, add yeast and milk mixture and blend to a soft dough. Knead on a floured surface for 10 minutes, adding more flour to make a soft, pliable dough. Leave to rise in a greased and covered bowl for about 1 hour or until doubled. Shape into 12 to 14 rounds on a well-floured baking sheet or plate. Pour enough oil to come half way up the sides of the biscuits into a large, deep frying pan. When temperature reaches 375°F drop in about 4 biscuits at a time. Fry on both sides until golden and puffy. Drain on paper towels. Biscuits can be kept warm in a moderate oven.

Variation: The dough makes good English muffins, too. Shape into 4 inch rounds and flatten slightly. Lightly grease the frying pan. When hot, fry rounds on both sides until golden and cooked through.

Parker House Rolls

Boston's famous Parker House Hotel gave its name to these white dinner rolls. They're brushed with butter, then folded into their characteristic shape. They freeze well, so they're perfect to make ahead for holidays.

1¹/₂ cups milk
3 tbsp sugar
2 tsps salt
¹/₂ cup vegetable shortening
2 pkgs active dry yeast
¹/₂ cup warm water
2 eggs
6–7 cups all-purpose flour
softened butter
(makes 24)

Preheat oven to 350°F. Scald the milk and combine with the sugar, salt, and shortening. Cool to lukewarm. Dissolve the yeast in the water and stir into the milk mixture. Beat in the eggs. Add half of the flour and stir until the dough is smooth. Work in the remaining flour just until a soft, but not sticky, dough is formed. Knead on a floured surface until smooth and elastic, about 10 minutes.

Place in a greased bowl, cover, and leave to rise in a warm place until doubled. Punch down, knead lightly, then roll out to ¹/₂ inch thick. Cut into 3 inch rounds with a floured cookie cutter. Spread each on one side with softened butter and score with the back of a knife just slightly off center. Fold the small part over the larger and press edges to seal. Place on greased baking sheets about 1 inch apart. Cover loosely and leave to rise again until almost doubled. Bake about 15 to 20 minutes or until nicely browned.

Muffins

These delicious quick breads have become very popular in recent years. Even the French have given them their seal of approval! Very often they're sweet, but these are savory with the taste of sharp cheese and wholegrain mustard.

2 cups all-purpose flour
1 tbsp baking powder
1 tbsp sugar
1/2 tsp salt
1/2 cup grated Cheddar cheese
1 egg
1 cup milk
1/4 cup margarine, melted
1 1/2 tsps wholegrain mustard
(12 muffins)

Preheat oven to 400°F and grease a 12-cup muffin pan. Combine flour, baking powder, sugar, salt, and cheese in a large bowl. Toss to mix well. Make a well in the middle. Mix egg, milk, margarine, and mustard and pour into the middle. Mix until dry ingredients are just moistened. Batter should be lumpy.

Fill the muffin cups about 2/3 full and bake 20 to 25 minutes, or until risen and golden brown. Tops will look peaked. Remove immediately from the pan.

Variations: Omit mustard and use 1 tablespoon chopped herbs. Use 1 cup wholewheat flour in place of the same amount of white flour and decrease baking powder to 2 teaspoons.

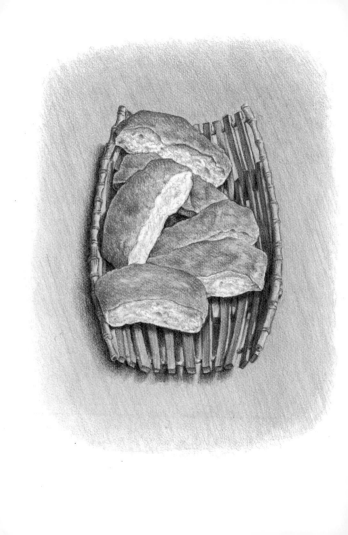

Ciabatta

An Italian bread made with olive oil which gives it an open texture, a crisp crust, and a completely different taste from any other bread. It makes delicious garlic bread and it's the perfect accompaniment to an antipasto.

1 pkg fast action yeast
1 tsp sugar
1 tsp salt
3¼ cups all-purpose flour
¾ cup warm water
½ cup warm olive oil
(1 loaf)

Preheat oven to 400°F. Combine yeast, sugar, salt, and flour in a large bowl. Mix water and olive oil and pour into the dry ingredients. Mix just until the ingredients come together. Knead, adding more flour as necessary. The dough should still look rough and slightly lumpy after kneading. Shape into an oblong loaf without making the top too smooth. Place on a greased baking sheet. Brush the top with more olive oil and cover loosely. Leave to rise about 1 hour in a warm place. Sprinkle lightly with flour. Bake bread about 25 to 30 minutes or until the loaf sounds hollow on the bottom when tapped.

Corn Bread

This quick bread doesn't need yeast to make it rise. It's become almost synonymous with Southern cooking, but it's just as much at home as an accompaniment to any good country style meal.

1 cup yellow cornmeal
1 cup all-purpose flour
4 tsps baking powder
1 tsp salt
2 tbsp sugar
¼ cup corn oil
1 large egg, beaten
1 cup milk
(1 loaf or 12 muffins)

Preheat oven to 425°F. Grease an 8 inch square pan or a 12-cup muffin pan. Mix the dry ingredients together and make a well in the middle. Pour in the oil and add the egg and milk. Mix with a fork until the ingredients are just moistened. Pour immediately into the prepared pan and bake about 20 to 25 minutes for the square pan and 15 to 20 minutes for muffins. The top will be light brown and feel springy to the touch. Serve warm with butter.

Variations: Add 2 crumbled rashers of cooked bacon or 4 tablespoons grated cheese or 1 tablespoon chopped herbs.

Popovers

These probably owe their existence to English Yorkshire pudding. Except for the addition of melted butter, the recipe ingredients are the same. Popovers look impressive, but they're very easy to make.

1 cup milk
1 tbsp melted butter
1 cup all-purpose flour
¹/₄ tsp salt
butter for greasing
(8 popovers)

Preheat oven to 450°F. Mix milk, melted butter, flour, and salt. Mix by hand, with an electric mixer, or a food processor, but only until batter is just smooth. Grease 8 muffin cups or ramekins very well and fill about ³/₄ full with batter. Bake 15 minutes, then lower the oven temperature to 350°F. Bake for a further 20 minutes, but don't open the oven door. Check after that time to make sure the popovers are firm. If not, bake a further 5 minutes or more. Make a small slit in the side to allow steam to escape. Remove immediately from the pan or ramekins and serve hot.

Variations: Add ¹/₂ cup grated cheese and a pinch of cayenne pepper. Sprinkle the greased cups with grated Parmesan cheese before filling with batter.

Peanut Butter and Jelly Buns

Combine two favorite flavors in a quick batter to bake in a muffin pan. Delicious for breakfast, great for snacks, or with a fresh fruit salad.

3/4 cup crunchy peanut butter
4 tbsps margarine
2 cups all-purpose flour
2 tsps baking powder
1/2 tsp salt
1/2 cup light brown sugar
1 egg, beaten
1 cup milk
4 tbsps grape, or other flavor jelly
(12 buns)

Preheat oven to 375°F. Grease a 12-cup muffin pan. Beat peanut butter and margarine until light. Add flour, baking powder, salt, and sugar and stir until mixture resembles coarse crumbs. Stir in egg and milk, adding a little more milk if needed to make a mixture like pancake batter.

Fill cups 1/3 full, then add a teaspoonful jelly. Cover with more batter to fill cups by 2/3. Bake immediately for about 20 to 25 minutes or until risen and golden brown. To test, stick a skewer into the middle and it should come out with no raw batter sticking to it. Remove from the pans at once and cool completely before serving.

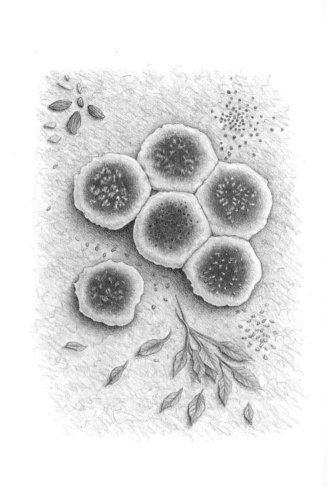

Pull-Aparts

Coat balls of dough in savory mixtures, then stick them together to form a loaf. To eat, just pull off your own freshly baked roll.

2¹/₂ cups all-purpose flour
2 cups wholewheat flour
4 tsps fast action yeast
2 tsps sugar
1 tsp salt
1 cup warm milk
¹/₂ cup warm water
2 eggs
Coating mixtures:
5 tbsps melted butter
chopped herbs, poppy seeds, grated cheese,
sesame seeds, ground nuts
(12 rolls)

Preheat oven to 400°F. Place white and wholewheat flours in separate bowls. Add 2 teaspoons yeast, 1 teaspoon sugar, and ¹/₂ teaspoon salt to each bowl. Mix milk and water and add half to each bowl. Add one egg to each bowl. Stir to make soft doughs. Knead each on a floured surface for about 10 minutes. Divide doughs into pieces and shape into smooth balls. Dip each ball in melted butter then into one of the remaining ingredients. Use as many different ones as you like. Pile the balls loosely in an ungreased angel food cake pan, alternating white and wholewheat doughs and coatings. Cover and leave to rise in a warm place until doubled, about 1 hour.

Bake for about 10 minutes, then lower the temperature to 350°F for about 30 minutes. Invert the pan on a cooking rack. The loaf will fall out naturally. Serve warm.

Old-fashioned Cinnamon Raisin Bread

Warm from the oven spread with butter or toasted for breakfast, this bread is absolutely delicious. What's more, it makes great ham sandwiches!

1 cup milk
4 tbsps margarine
4 tbsps brown sugar
1/2 cup warm water
2 pkgs active dry yeast
3 cups all-purpose flour
1–2 cups wholewheat flour
1 tsp salt
2 tsps cinnamon
1 egg, beaten
1 cup raisins
(2 loaves)

Preheat oven to 375°F. Scald milk and stir in margarine and sugar until dissolved. Cool to lukewarm. Mix the water with the yeast. Mix white flour and 1 cup of wholewheat flour with the salt and cinnamon in a large bowl. Make a well in the middle and add the egg and the milk and yeast mixtures. Beat until completely blended. Add enough of the remaining wholewheat flour to make a soft dough. Knead for about 10 minutes working in more flour, if necessary. Place in a greased bowl, cover, and leave to rise in a warm place until doubled in bulk, about 1½ hours. Punch down the dough and knead in the raisins. Grease two 9 x 5 inch loaf pans. Divide dough and shape into two loaves. Place in the pans, cover and leave about 30 minutes to rise again. Bake about 35 to 40 minutes until tops sound hollow when tapped. Cool on wire racks. May be frozen for up to 4 months.

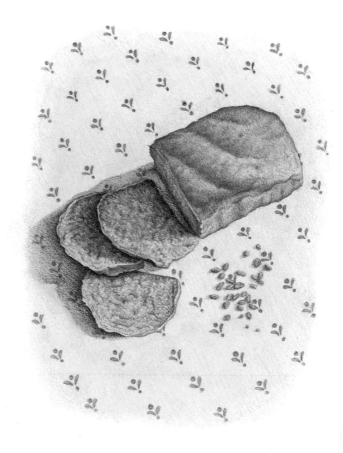

Oatmeal Bread

Make this bread with half wholewheat and half white flour if you want an even healthier loaf. Fast action yeast cuts the rising time in half and makes mixing very easy.

2³/₄ cups all-purpose flour
1 cup quick oats
1 pkg fast action yeast
¹/₂ tsp salt
1 tbsp sugar
1 tbsp margarine, melted
1 cup warm milk
¹/₄ cup warm water
(1 loaf)

Preheat oven to 350°F. Mix flour, oats, yeast, salt, and sugar in a large bowl. Combine margarine, milk and water and pour into the dry ingredients. Mix until well blended. Add more flour, if necessary to make a soft dough. Knead about 10 minutes on a floured surface and shape into a loaf. Grease one 9 x 5 inch loaf pan and place in the dough. Cover and leave to rise until almost to the top of the pan. Brush the top of the loaf with a little milk and sprinkle lightly with more oats. Bake about 40 minutes. Remove from the pan and cool on a wire rack.

Everyday White Bread

A basic white bread that's inexpensive to make and invaluable for sandwiches or toast anytime. Make two loaves, one for now and one to freeze for later.

3¹/₃ cups warm water
2 pkgs active dry yeast
3 tbsps vegetable shortening, melted
3 tbsps sugar
9–10 cups all-purpose flour
2 tsps salt
melted margarine
(2 loaves)

Preheat oven to 425°F. Mix ³/₄ cup of the warm water with the yeast and leave to dissolve. Mix remaining water with the shortening and sugar. Mix all but 1 cup of the flour and salt and make a well in the middle. Pour in the yeast and other liquid ingredients and mix to a soft dough, adding additional flour, as needed. Knead on a floured surface until smooth and elastic, about 10 minutes. Place in a greased bowl, cover and leave to rise in a warm place until doubled in bulk.

Punch down and shape into two loaves. Grease two 9 x 5 inch loaf pans and place in the dough. Brush with melted margarine, cover and leave to rise again until almost to the tops of the pans, about 40 minutes. Bake about 30 to 35 minutes or until golden brown and loaves sound hollow when tapped. Remove from the pans and cool on wire racks. Freeze up to 6 months.

Wholewheat Bread

A hearty, healthy loaf made with half wholewheat and half white flour for a lighter texture. It has yogurt and honey in it, too, for extra goodness. If you want a very substantial loaf, increase the proportion of wholewheat. If you use all wholewheat flour, add about half an envelope of extra yeast to help it rise.

1½ cups warm water	*4 cups wholewheat flour*
2 pkgs active dry yeast	*4 cups all-purpose flour*
1 cup plain yogurt,	*2 tsps salt*
at room temperature	*melted margarine*
3 tbsps vegetable oil	*bran*
3 tbsps honey	

(2 loaves)

Preheat oven to 425°F. Mix warm water with the yeast and leave to dissolve. Mix yoghurt, oil and honey and add to the yeast. Combine both flours and salt in a large bowl and make a well in the middle.

Pour in the yeast mixture and mix to a soft dough, adding additional white or wholewheat flour, if needed. Knead on a floured surface until smooth and elastic, about 10 minutes. Place in a greased bowl, cover and leave to rise in a warm place until doubled in bulk. The greater the percentage of wholewheat flour, the longer the dough will take to rise.

Punch down and shape into two loaves. Grease two 9 x 5 inch loaf pans and place in the dough. Brush with melted margarine, cover and leave to rise again until almost to the tops of the pans, about 40 minutes. Sprinkle loaves with a little bran, if desired.

Bake about 30 to 35 minutes or until golden brown and loaves sound hollow when tapped. Remove from the pans and cool on wire racks. Freeze for up to 6 months.

Banana Rye Bread

Don't dismiss the idea until you've tried it! This is an old-fashioned recipe from New England, and it's undeniably an unusual combination. Try it spread with cream cheese or with the suggested sandwich filling.

1 pkg active dry yeast
1¹/₂ tbsps warm water
1¹/₂ tsps salt
2 tsps sugar
1¹/₂ tbsps melted vegetable shortening
3 small ripe bananas, mashed
1¹/₄–1¹/₂ cups rye flour
¹/₄–1¹/₂ cups all-purpose flour
(1 loaf)

Preheat oven to 350°F. Dissolve yeast in warm water. Combine the salt, sugar, shortening, and bananas in a large bowl. Add the yeast and the rye flour and beat until smooth. Stir in enough of the white flour to make a firm dough. Knead on a floured surface for about 10 minutes until smooth and not sticky. Place in a greased bowl and leave in a warm place to rise for about 1 hour or until doubled.

Punch down the dough and divide it in three pieces. Roll each to a thick rope. Starting in the middle, braid the three ropes working to one end and then the other. Tuck the ends under. Grease one 9 x 5 inch loaf pan and place in the braided loaf, tucking the ends in further, if necessary. Leave in a warm place to rise again until about doubled.

Bake 35 to 45 minutes. Turn out immediately onto a wire rack to cool.

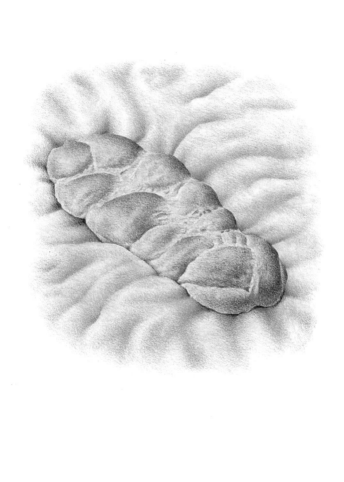

Boston Brown Bread

Purists say this bread is the only correct accompaniment to Boston Baked Beans. It's steamed, rather than baked, but you won't need any special equipment, just a large saucepan, some foil and some empty coffee cans.

1 cup wholewheat flour
1 cup cornmeal
1 cup rye flour
1 tsp salt
2 tsps baking soda
³/₄ cup molasses
2 cups buttermilk
1 cup chopped dates
(2 loaves)

Grease two clean 1 lb coffee cans. Combine all the ingredients and divide between the two cans, filling them ²/₃ full. Cover the cans tightly with two layers of foil. Place the cans on a rack in a large deep pan, casserole dish, or roasting pan with a cover. You can use a cooling rack balanced on heatproof ramekins if you don't have a steamer rack. Pour in boiling water to come up to the level of the rack. Cover the pan and bring to the boil. Keep the water boiling gently, adding more as needed during steaming. Steam about 3 hours or until a skewer inserted into the middle of the breads comes out clean. Loosen the sides and remove from the cans immediately. Cut with a serrated knife. Serve warm with butter or cream cheese.

Index